The Illawarra

BETWEEN THE MOUNTAINS AND THE SEA

Revisited

Photography by SUE and BRIAN KENDRICK

Text by GILLIAN CUMMING

A Lightstorm Publication

Published by Lightstorm Publishing ©
Distributed by Lightstorm Photography
PO Box 1167 Nowra NSW 2541
Ph: (02) 4446 0911 Fax: (02) 4446 0922

First published December 2003
© Photographs: Sue and Brian Kendrick 2003
© Text: Gillian Cumming 2003

ISBN 0-9586745-4-X

Title Page: The unforgettable sight of Wollongong, viewed from Bulli Lookout. Wollongong and Port Kembla - the industrial area for which the region is well known - can be seen in the distance.
Right: Sunrise, Kiama Harbour.
Below: Stuart Park, North Wollongong.
Overleaf (clockwise from top left): Kiama's famous painted cow, outside the Old Fire Station Community Arts Centre; houses hug the ocean cliffs at the northern beachside suburbs of Scarborough and Wombarra; a surfer enjoys a great wave at Werri Beach Gerringong; aerial view of Port Kembla Harbour; the Little Blowhole, Kiama; Wollongong saltwater sea-pool.

CONTENTS

INTRODUCTION

The name Illawarra is derived from the language of the local Aboriginal people, who came from north of Australia sometime between 20,000 and 40,000 years ago. Although it has had a mixture of meanings over the years, it is generally regarded as describing a pleasant place near the sea.

The Illawarra's 1128 square kilometres comprise the local government areas of Wollongong, Shellharbour and Kiama. Home to more than 270,000 people, the region snakes along 85 kilometres of the New South Wales coastline from the Royal National Park in the north to Kiama in the south. To the west, the Illawarra is flanked by the magnificent escarpment that becomes the Southern Tableland, while beyond to the south lies the Shoalhaven district.

Lake Illawarra is an impressive focal point for the region. Bounded by Wollongong in the north and Shellharbour in the south, the natural saltwater lagoon is a haven for fish and birdlife and a popular spot for fishing and watersports.

Explorers George Bass and Matthew Flinders became the first Europeans to visit the region when they accidentally landed the 'Tom Thumb' at Towradgi Beach in 1796. The Illawarra's coal potential was discovered soon afterwards, but difficulties with access to the region meant it was timber and not black coal that finally led Europeans to settle here. Pastoralists followed in 1815 when Liverpool farmer Dr. Charles Throsby hacked a route across the Southern Tableland in search of feed for his drought-stricken cattle. Grazing, cropping and dairying thrived and the Illawarra became known as the 'Garden of New South Wales'.

By the mid-1800's, collieries had been developed in the region's coal-rich north and north-west, boosting the development of business and government infrastructure around the settlement of Wollongong. Industrial development followed early last century when Charles Hoskins' iron and steel works began production in 1931.

Left: A place of beauty and history, Wollongong Harbour's stone walls offer protection to both pleasure craft and the town's commercial fishing fleet. Overlooking the harbour at Flagstaff Point is Wollongong Lighthouse, erected in 1937 to warn passing ships of the dangers of Bellambi Reef to the north and the Five Islands to the south.

ILLAWARRA REGION

Hoskins' dream led to the creation of BHP (Broken Hill Proprietary Co Ltd), now the world's largest diversified miner. Once known internationally as 'the Big Australian', a 2001 merger transformed the company into the $60 billion mega-mining company BHP Billiton Ltd, which in the Illawarra continues to be based at Wollongong's industrial heartland of Port Kembla.

The people of the Illawarra come from more than 80 countries, making the region the most ethnically diverse non-metropolitan area in Australia.

The region's beauty has captured the imaginations of artists and writers, from Eugene von Guérard's pastoral plains and lush rainforests painted in the mid-1800's to contemporary talents such as painter John Vander and playwright Wendy Richardson. The Illawarra also nurtured the talents of aviation pioneer Lawrence Hargrave, who late in the 19th century carried out his box-kite experiments on Stanwell Park Beach.

The region's educational facilities are led by the University of Wollongong, which is ranked among the top five universities nationally, and Illawarra sportspeople shine on the world stage in areas such as surfing, cricket and golf.

Whereas Wollongong has developed into the industrial and commercial powerhouse of the region, Shellharbour is now a thriving residential and water recreational area while seaside Kiama, with its famous blowhole, is regarded as a tourist mecca.

Recreationally, the Illawarra has something for everyone - fishing, surfing, sailing, bushwalking, hang-gliding and cycling. As a result, tourism is a powerful economic force as people discover the Illawarra's diverse, natural beauty.

The Illawarra - best kept secret in New South Wales!

Left: Cabbage palms are a feature of the Illawarra landscape, particularly in the dairy farming areas of Rose Valley and Jamberoo.

HISTORY

ABORIGINAL HISTORY

Some time during the last Ice Age, between 20,000 and 40,000 years ago, when Borneo, Java and South-East Asia were linked, dark-skinned people made their way to the Australian continent.

Traditionally hunters and gatherers, these indigenous people moved in small tribes to where food was plentiful. Before long, the coastal Illawarra's fertile soil, lush vegetation and abundance of food was supporting growing numbers of Aborigines. The obstacle of the Great Divide is thought to have prevented Illawarra Aborigines moving to higher lands, where food was harder to find and indigenous populations were smaller.

By the time Europeans set foot in the Illawarra there were five coastal Aboriginal tribes. Nomadic and semi-nomadic, from north to south they were known as the Dharawal, Wadi Wadi, Gurandad, Dharumba and Wandandian people.

They moved to where native foods were seasonal or where religious, social or ceremonial needs dictated. Sometimes this meant travelling long distances and the trails created were later used by Europeans and sometimes became roads.

The names Illawarra and Wollongong, along with many other place names used today, are derived from the oral languages of the region's Aboriginal population. The word Illawarra is meant to convey 'a pleasant place' or 'a high and pleasant place near the sea', while Wollongong is thought to mean hard or high ground near water. It has also been explained as the sound of waves breaking on sand and as a derivative of the name of an early Aborigine, Woolonglow, whose descendants continue to live locally.

Aborigines were bound by kinship and religion. Marriage occurred with someone from outside a clan and men could have more than one wife. While men were responsible for social, political and religious

Left: Bushrangers Bay, Bass Point. Excavation of shell middens at Bass Point have revealed much about the diet and lifestyle of the area's original inhabitants.

customs, women cared for their immediate family and provided most of the food needs. Men hunted with spears hafted with chips of quartz and fished using multi-pronged bone-tipped spears. They often fished the coast at night with torches fashioned from beaten and tied bark and would drag bream from shallows with their hands. Women fished with shell hook and line and gathered vegetable matter, shellfish, small mammals and reptiles.

Nature provided not only the food needs of the indigenous population, but all their requirements for living. Bark was cut from trees to make canoes and overhanging rocks provided shelter, which Aborigines marked with drawings or paintings in charcoal and ochre. Tools included boomerangs, spears and digging sticks as well as fishing lines, hooks and multi-pronged fishing spears made from stone, shell, bone, hair and plant material. In winter, possum skins were worn to keep warm while for decoration head bands of kangaroo teeth were worn and bones were pushed through men's noses. The temperate climate and abundant food supply of the region are thought to have offered the Illawarra's indigenous population a good lifestyle.

Middens of the shell remains of Aboriginal tribes' basic diet can be found around Lake Illawarra, Bass Point and other locations across the region. Excavation of these middens, as well as the uncovering of campsites and the discovery of shelters adorned with engravings, drawings and paintings, has revealed valuable information about the diet and lifestyle of the original inhabitants. Illawarra engravings have been found to represent humans, birds, fish and mythological figures.

Following European contact and settlement, traditional tribal life was progressively eroded as the indigenous people's social and economic systems fell apart and introduced diseases such as small pox, influenza, measles and syphilis took their toll. It is estimated that there were about 3000 full-blood Aborigines in the Illawarra in 1820, but by the turn of the 20th century only a handful remained. Descendants of these traditional tribal Aborigines, people who prize their heritage and maintain certain traditions, live in the Illawarra today.

EXPLORATION AND SETTLEMENT

The first sighting of the Illawarra by Europeans is thought to have occurred from afar in 1770 when Captain James Cook was heading north to where his landing of the Endeavour took place at Botany Bay. Cook almost set foot on land near Woonona, today a suburb north of Wollongong, but his landing party was defeated by rough sea. The party did, however, observe a small number of dark-skinned people on the shore edge and Cook noted in his log a landmark he named Red Point, thought to be Port Kembla. He also described as 'the crown of a hat' a landmark believed to be Mount Kembla.

Many ships sailed past over the ensuing years, but the Illawarra remained largely unexplored by Europeans, mainly because the region lacked a natural harbour. Also, the mountain range to the west was a natural barrier, too difficult for settlers to penetrate. It wasn't until a quarter of a century after Cook's sail past that explorers George Bass and Matthew Flinders accidentally landed in the region in 1796. While searching for Port Hacking, their small boat Tom Thumb was blown further south and eventually washed ashore somewhere near Towradgi, south of Cook's attempted Woonona landing. Afterwards, Bass and Flinders entered Lake Illawarra, naming it Tom Thumb Lagoon, although a lagoon north of Port Kembla was given that name erroneously some time later.

The following year the region received some unexpected visitors - survivors of the shipwrecked Sydney Cove. From a party of 17 that set out from near Cape Everard in Victoria, bound for Sydney Town, only three members were rescued by Sydney fishermen, who noticed the

Left: This evocative bronze statue honouring the region's coal mining heritage was created by local sculptor Liz Johnson. Depicting a contemporary miner with his brother of yesteryear, the monument was erected in 1995 outside Wollongong Council offices.

Above right: The first recorded visit by Europeans to the Illawarra occurred when explorers Bass and Flinders accidentally landed near Towradgi in 1796 while searching for Port Hacking. This re-enactment, by members of Theatre South, commemorated the bicentenary of Bass and Flinders' historic voyage in the 'Tom Thumb'.

Right: Large spreading fig trees and historic stonewalls characterise the dairy farming country in the south of the region.

smoke of a coal fire near Coalcliff. Later that year George Bass returned to investigate the region's coal potential. He reported observing several seams of coal in the towering cliffs buttressing the ocean, but the difficulty of transporting coal from an isolated region to Sydney proved too great and the Illawarra remained largely undisturbed.

Eight years later, in 1805, it was timber and not black coal that ultimately led to the region's settlement after Government surveyor James Meehan reported that dense cedar forests stood in the Illawarra. Still, it wasn't until 1812 that cedar cutters began to arrive, cutting large trees into planks that were carried or pulled to the top of Bulli where they were hauled by bullock to Parramatta then on to Sydney. Later, cedar was hauled to the beach and onto boats bound for Sydney.

By 1815, graziers had begun driving cattle into the Illawarra. Leading the way was Liverpool farmer Dr Charles Throsby, who hacked a route across the tableland in search of feed for his drought-stricken cattle. Looking over the Illawarra from the escarpment, he was not disappointed by the green vista before him. The following year Governor Lachlan Macquarie directed that Crown land be reserved and land grants be established.

As red cedar continued to be taken from the region, settlers moved in and established farms. By 1826, the settlement close to where boats were anchored became known as Wollongong. Three years later soldiers were stationed there to control illegal cedar cutting, warn off bushrangers and escaped convicts, prevent degradation of the indigenous population and protect settlers.

Local Government began operation in 1843 when Governor Gipps established the Illawarra District Council, which had responsibilities as far south as the Shoalhaven River. That same year, the introduction of clearing leases enabled pioneer Caroline Chisholm to settle immigrants on fertile land in Shellharbour. Grazing was eventually overtaken by cropping and dairying, which produced grain, vegetables and butter for the Sydney market. The following year the opening of Bulli Pass

Left: Built in 1939 in the Elizabethan Revival style, historic Gleniffer Brae was the family home of Sidney Hoskins, father of steel-making in the Illawarra. Designed by architect Geoffrey Loveridge, the Keiraville manor house later served as a private girls' school but is now home to the Conservatorium of Music.

improved road access between Sydney and the Illawarra and created a breathtaking entry to the region.

By the mid-1800's, the supply of cedar was almost exhausted and agriculture was becoming of secondary importance to the development of the region's greatest natural asset - high-grade black coal. Spurred by the success of James Schoobert, who in 1849 succeeded in opening the region's first coal mine at Mt Keira, Wollongong shifted from being a busy farming community towards becoming the industrial giant it is today. By 1880, ten coal pits were being worked around Wollongong and mining villages had begun to mushroom northwards. But despite the advent of coal, in the outlying areas of Shellharbour and Kiama dairying continued to flourish and in the 1880's the region was regarded as the 'Garden of New South Wales'.

The completion of the Illawarra rail line in 1888 proved crucial to the region's trade and progress. Locals and visitors were no longer dependent on ship transport or on having to negotiate the terrible roads and mountainous approaches by coach and cart. Overnight, access to the Illawarra had become relatively easy and visitors from Sydney soon discovered the pleasures of the region's scenic beauty. The upgrading of Wollongong Harbour in 1895 and the creation, more than 30 years later, of a large deep-water harbour at Port Kembla served to support the region's burgeoning industrial base.

By the early 1930's Charles Hoskins' iron and steel works had commenced production of steel on land west of Port Kembla. In 1935 the company was sold to the Broken Hill Propriety Company (BHP) and an ambitious program of expansion followed.

In the post-war economic boom of the 1950's the Illawarra began a change of face. The region's predominantly Anglo-Irish appearance was changed by an influx of thousands of European migrants. Today the Illawarra's population is made up of people from more than 80 countries worldwide.

While the Illawarra remains known around the world for its progressive industrial base, there is a noticeable transformation taking place within its towns as ageing baby boomers move into the region - Australia's largest commuter corridor - in search of a coastal lifestyle sea change. This paints a bright picture for the Illawarra as it moves confidently into the 21st century.

THE NATURAL ENVIRONMENT

Black coal might be the Illawarra's most valuable natural asset but, economics aside, residents and visitors to the Illawarra are more likely to favour the region's emerald green forests, lush parks and gardens and countless golden beaches and waterways.

The Illawarra is straddled by green corridors and laced by national parks, state forests and tracts of privately held escarpment land. Eastwards, the region's lowland kisses the Pacific Ocean at beaches and rocky outcrops that curve along more than 85 kilometres of coastline.

To the south, Lake Illawarra is a haven for watersports and, bordering Kiama, the Minnamurra River is an important water habitat and fish nursery, also popular with anglers. Bound by Wollongong in the north and Shellharbour on its southern shores, Lake Illawarra is the largest body of water in the region. Like most of NSW's coastal saltwater lagoons, it is broad and shallow. While its maximum depth is 3.5 metres, there are extensive shallows of less than one metre. The 35 square kilometre lake is a haven for fish and birdlife and attracts water-based recreational activities such as fishing, prawning, sailing, sailboarding, water skiing, canoeing and paddleboating. Initiatives by the Lake Illawarra Authority have markedly improved the lake's water quality and transformed its foreshore into attractive recreational areas.

Many creeks and waterways across the region snake their way from high in the escarpment down to the ocean. The Minnamurra River in Kiama is the largest river in the region. Its mangrove-lined banks and natural vegetation are an important breeding place for water birds and its watery depths make an ideal fish nursery.

Killalea in Shellharbour is among the region's least disturbed freshwater wetlands, while small coastal lagoons such as Spring Creek at Bombo and Werri Lagoon at Gerroa are important habitat for water birds and popular picnic spots.

Previous pages: The sea-side saltwater pool at Bellambi is one of nearly twenty such pools dotted along the region's coastline from Coalcliff to Gerroa.
Left: Cathedral Rocks is situated 3kms north of Kiama, at the southern end of Jones Beach. This distinctive volcanic rock, formed more than 250 million years ago, has lured visitors since 1890.
Above right: The region's many wetlands, including Lake Illawarra and the Minnamurra River, support a variety of birdlife, including the ubiquitous pelican.
Right: A coastal walking track wanders the along coastline from Kiama to the seaside towns of Gerringong and Gerroa further south.

The regeneration of Tom Thumb Lagoon, adjacent to Australia's Industry World, has resulted in the return to the wetland of native flora and fauna. Adjacent to Port Kembla is Five Islands: Big Island, Flinders Islet, Bass Islet, Martin Islet and Rocky Islet - important habitat and breeding sites for sea birds.

Illawarra's lakes, rivers and waterways support a vast range of birdlife, including more than 20 species of migratory bird, some rare. Waterfowls, swans and pelicans are commonly seen across the region, along with grey teal, grebes, black cormorants, egrets, ibis, spoonbills, herons, sea eagles, stilt, curlews and reed warblers.

Sheltered rock pools and swimming holes, along with seaside salt-water pools, dot the coastline. The sheltered waters of Bushrangers Bay Aquatic Reserve at Bass Point, south of Shellharbour, feature diverse underwater habitats and are favoured by snorkellers and scuba divers. The pristine bay's shallow waters harbour more than 35 species of fish as well as oysters, shellfish and other marine life.

Surfing hot spots include 'The Farm', Mystics Beach, South Shellharbour Beach and Killalea Beach, while for swimmers patrolled beaches dot the coastline from Stanwell Park in the north to Werri Beach in the south.

The Illawarra is bordered by the Royal National Park in the north and Seven Mile Beach National Park in the south. In between, the region is dotted with many parks and gardens. The escarpment, a stunning backdrop to the region, rises abruptly from the Pacific Ocean, climbing to more than 300 metres in the north and over twice this elevation west of Kiama. Dominating the Illawarra landscape, its cliffs and plateau are comprised of massive beds of durable quartz sandstone. Beneath the cliffs, weaker claystone tends to erode and undermine the sandstone, sometimes causing the cliffs to collapse.

The escarpment is used by bushwalkers, rock climbers, abseilers, paragliders and hang-gliders. Lookouts at Stanwell Tops, Sublime Point, Mount Keira and Mount Kembla provide breath-taking panoramas. Nestled into the side of the escarpment at leafy Mount Pleasant in Wollongong is Rhododendron Park, where thousands of varieties of rhododendron and azalea thrive in cool, moist conditions to create magnificent mass-colour shows in spring.

Wollongong's green corridor includes the beautiful Botanic Garden edging the escarpment at Keiraville, plus its annexes Mt Keira Summit Park, Korrungulla Wetlands at Primbee, Kelly's Falls at Stanwell Tops, Wodi Wodi Walking Trail at Stanwell Park and Puckey's Estate on the

Right: Corrimal Beach.

foreshore at North Wollongong. The Botanic Garden is host to plants from dry and wet tropical areas and temperate climates. Popular with locals and visitors is the sunken rose garden where 2000 rose shrubs bloom annually.

The 20-hectare Puckey's Estate is one of only two remnant hind dune lagoon complexes between Port Hacking and Lake Illawarra. Its diverse vegetation and closeness to Wollongong's CBD makes Puckey's an area of significance to be preserved.

Shellharbour's Macquarie Pass National Park covers 1000 hectares, 10 kilometres west of suburban Albion Park. Fed by Macquarie Rivulet, the park harbours magnificent sub-tropical rainforest and superb waterfalls. There are walking tracks, several natural swimming pools and three picnic areas, including Clover Hill overlooking Macquarie Falls.

Also within Shellharbour is the 250-hectare Blackbutt Reserve, the Illawarra's last remaining tract of coastal plain forest. The reserve is a popular venue for walking and get-togethers and has barbecue facilities, a playground and an open-air amphitheatre.

The Killalea State Recreation Area curves along the coastline from Bass Point to Kiama. Aboriginal middens as well as one of the Illawarra's few littoral rainforest areas lie within this important reserve.

The 400-hectare Minnamurra Rainforest, Australia's southernmost sub-tropical rainforest, is only a 10-minute drive from Jamberoo. Part of the Budderoo National Park, the award-winning microcosm is accessible via a boardwalk that enables viewing of the rainforest for young, old and disabled. Visitors can make the two-hour return walk to Minnamurra Falls, from where the rainforest canopy can also be viewed. A sanctuary for native lyrebirds, which are commonly seen and heard, Minnamurra also supports populations of honeyeaters, King parrots, kookaburras and yellow-throated scrub wrens. Reptiles include the red-bellied black snake and diamond python and there are colonies of platypus, eels and crayfish. This rare tract of sub-tropical rainforest is also a habitat for more than 120 vegetative species of plant life, and red cedars that survived the early timber cutters are among the biggest trees.

Left: Located within Budderoo National Park the spectacular Minnamurra Falls can be viewed while on a loop walk. After following the Minnamurra Rainforest boardwalk, a steep climb leads to a viewing platform where the 42m-high lower falls and the 20m-high upper falls (pictured here) can be observed.

Above right: Wollongong's special relationship with sister city Kawasaki was commemorated in 1993 with this gift - a 10 m-long traditional Japanese bridge built by Kawasaki craftsmen in the grounds of the Wollongong Botanic Garden.

Right: Bellambi Lagoon, an important water-bird breeding ground and sanctuary.

A REGIONAL VIEW

One of the Illawarra's greatest assets is its geographic diversity. Backdropped by the magnificent escarpment, there are few places in the Illawarra that do not afford breathtaking vistas of emerald green hillsides, inland waters or ocean beaches. In fact, it's this spectacular meeting of mountain and sea that gives the region its special character and makes it irresistible to holidayers and locals alike.

Whereas Wollongong is the economic and industrial heartland of the region, it shares pockets of country quiet with its southern coastal neighbours of Shellharbour and Kiama, Gerringong and Gerroa, and the sleepy hinterland village of Jamberoo.

WOLLONGONG

Situated 80 kilometres south of Sydney, the City of Wollongong stretches for more than 60 kilometres along the coastline, from Helensburgh in the north to the shores of Lake Illawarra then Windang and Dapto in the south and south-west.

New South Wales' third-largest city after Sydney and Newcastle, Wollongong is by far the Illawarra's largest population centre with 191,000 people.

It was cedar, not coal, that attracted Europeans to the Illawarra in 1812 and eventually led to Wollongong's settlement. After dense cedar forests were felled for the Sydney timber market, graziers and settlers moved in to establish farms on cleared land. By 1826, the coastal settlement known as Wollongong was producing meat, vegetables and dairy products for local and Sydney markets.

Although black coal was first sighted in the ocean cliffs of the north during the closing years of the 19th century, the region's inaccessibility and the difficulty of transporting heavy raw materials to Sydney delayed mining. As a result, Wollongong remained a pioneering farming community until the mid-1800's when coal mining at last became viable and mining villages began to mushroom northwards. Today's suburbs of Helensburgh, Coalcliff, Coledale, Scarborough, Wombarra, Clifton and Bulli began life as villages settled close to coal mines. As their names suggest, early miners and their families who

Previous pages: A panoramic view of North Wollongong Beach and the northern Illawarra from the Wollongong Harbour breakwater.
Left: An aerial view of Stanwell Park and Coalcliff, with the Coalcliff Coke Works visible in the background. Pioneer aviator Lawrence Hargraves undertook his box kite experiments on Stanwell Park Beach in the late 19th Century.

lived in these villages had strong ties with England, Scotland, Ireland and Wales. Bulli's coal-mining past is preserved at its historic railway station, also the home of a mining museum displaying valuable artefacts.

Original miners' cottages - modest, quaint-looking dwellings that remain scattered through Wollongong's northern reaches and are often found perched precariously along the clifftops - are now sought-after real estate. Scarborough Hotel, located dramatically at the cliff's edge overlooking the Pacific Ocean, dates from this period and is a much-loved landmark.

The area's natural beauty was recognised from the early 1900's and led to the development of beachside Austinmer as one of New South Wales' first holiday resorts.

Bald Hill at Stanwell Park is prized as Wollongong's best lookout and is known internationally as a popular place for hang-gliding. A memorial also acknowledges Bald Hill as the birthplace of flight, as it was from here that aviation pioneer Lawrence Hargrave tested his innovative box kites early in the 20th century.

South of Austinmer, Thirroul, a name derived from the Aboriginal word Thurrural - thought to mean 'valley of the Cabbage Tree Palms' - began as a mining and rail town and is now a popular retreat for Sydneysiders and a haven for writers, artists and craftspeople.

Thirroul's greatest literary claim to fame dates back to 1922 when English novelist D.H. Lawrence wrote 'Kangaroo' while living at Wyewurk, a California-style bungalow with distinctive Australian federation features, from May to August of that year.

As industry continued to develop, the Illawarra's northern outposts eventually merged and Wollongong grew to become one of Australia's biggest industrial cities. Instrumental to this growth was the completion of the Illawarra rail line in 1888 and, early in the 20th century, the construction of a deep-sea port at Port Kembla.

Wollongong's reputation as a steel city is one that it proudly continues to nurture on the expanding international market. Increasingly, though, the city's sophisticated economy is also a reflection of rapid growth in the tertiary industries of education, advanced technology and tourism.

Left: A sunrise view of Austinmer from Brickyard Point.
Overleaf: The northern beachside suburbs of Austinmer and Thirroul.

Now Australia's eighth-largest city, Wollongong has a rich cultural life supported by a Conservatorium of Music and a vibrant theatre scene. The city's performers include singer Anthony Warlow and Australian Chamber Orchestra director Richard Tognetti. Wollongong City Gallery, Australia's largest regional art museum, is home to enviable collections of contemporary, Aboriginal and colonial art. Venues include the 500-seat Illawarra Performing Arts Centre and the 5500-seat WIN Entertainment Centre.

While Wollongong has all the amenities of contemporary, urban living, its lineal coastal development means that it has retained easy access to beaches and parks, forests and mountain. Treasured natural assets include Mount Keira, located high above the city, where locals and visitors trek to enjoy panoramic views from its lookout or indulge in hiking and rock climbing.

While the City of Wollongong stretches narrowly along the coastline covering 715 square kilometres, the heavy industry for which the city is mainly known is concentrated in the industrial heartland of Port Kembla, several kilometres south of the CBD.

Left: An aerial view of Bulli and Woonona.
Below: The sea-pool at Bulli.

The shape of industry in the Illawarra was decided back in the 1920's when visionary industrialist Charles Hoskins bought 162 hectares of land west of Port Kembla. Hoskins' iron and steel works eventually became Australian Iron and Steel, which in 1935 was sold to Broken Hill Proprietary Company Limited (BHP), now BHP Billiton. Built on reclaimed swampland, the gigantic industrial centre has its own deep-water port, which has been rated as one of Australia's most strategic heavy industry export points. Apart from handling massive amounts of coal, iron ore and steel - fed to the port by the steelworks and a string of collieries that mine the escarpment and mountain plateau to the north and west - the port's commercial strength has been boosted by its multi-million dollar grain-handling terminal.

Beyond the industrial precinct, Port Kembla beach is only minutes away and is a regular haunt for surfers. Further south, Lake Illawarra is a protected haven for natural vegetation and wildlife and a popular place to enjoy watersports. At the lake's northern entrance, Windang is the hub of boaties and anglers. To the south-west, many of the city's new residential developments are occurring at West Dapto.

Nestled into the escarpment is the beautiful historic village of Mount Kembla, where Australia's worst mining disaster occurred in 1902 when a gas explosion killed 95 men and boys. Home to the last weather-board hotel to be built in the Illawarra, dating back to 1896, Mount Kembla also boasts a lookout and is enjoyed by picnickers and bush-walkers. This idyllic outpost is now contributing to the region's industrial revitalisation through the opening in 2003 of the state-of-the-art Dendrobium coal mine - the first underground coal mine to open in these southern coalfields in more than 20 years.

Left: The breakwater light at Wollongong Harbour is one of only two cast iron and boiler plate lighthouses in Australia. Erected in 1871, the 13m-high lighthouse originally had an acetylene gas lamp before changing to electric light in 1916.
Above right: A flower seller on Wollongong's colourful pedestrian mall.
Right: The Illawarra is a vibrant multicultural community - people from more than 80 countries now call the Illawarra home. In 1960 Flaminio Fina left his native Italy to seek a new life in Australia and his sister Filomina followed in 1967. While working at the steelworks and later in his delicatessen, Flaminio dreamed of making pasta and in 1986 he opened 'Pasta Fina' in Crown Street. Flaminio's pasta has won numerous awards at the Royal Easter Show.
Overleaf: Twilight, Wollongong Harbour.

UNIVERSITY OF WOLLONGONG

Early last century Illawarra students had no choice but to travel to Sydney to further their education, as the region lacked tertiary and technical training facilities. The Illawarra's first trades school and technical college opened in North Wollongong in 1928 and by 1951 this establishment had become a division of the NSW University of Technology in Sydney. Ten years later it shifted gear to become the Wollongong College of the University of NSW. By 1962 the campus had been renamed Wollongong University College, noted for science and engineering courses geared towards the needs of the region's fast-developing heavy industry.

Soon afterwards, its course core expanded to include language, general studies and commerce. When the University of Wollongong was finally established in 1975 it became Australia's 18th university. Two years later the university had more than 2500 students and 150 academic staff. Enormous growth occurred during the 1980's and early 1990's, a period dubbed 'the McKinnon era' after its Vice Chancellor Ken McKinnon, whose stewardship resulted in an unprecedented 15 new buildings (now there are more than 90 permanent buildings) set within an idyllic, greenfield environment at the foot of Mt Keira. Today the award-winning university's three campuses and five access centres for nine faculties attract more than 18,000 students from around Australia and overseas.

Following the success of the main Wollongong campus, the university established a campus at Dubai in the United Arab Emirates in 1993 and a Shoalhaven campus was opened at Nowra in 2000.

A strong research focus, often in partnership with industry and government, has fostered eight research institutes and three Key Centres for Teaching and Research, including a State Centre of Excellence in Telecommunications. The university's other arms include an interactive Science Centre at Fairy Meadow, the Recreation and Aquatic Centre and a 20-hectare Innovation Campus, which is expected to be fully developed by 2013.

Left: An aerial view of the University of Wollongong campus, showing its proximity to the city centre, Port Kembla and the sea.
Above right: This composite photo captures one of the specialities of the Science Centre with its world class planetarium and observatory. The sculpture in the foreground is 'Cross Sections' - a representation of the Southern Cross.
Right: Cryolophosaurus (the frozen crested dinosaur) is the most complete and only large dinosaur found in Antarctica. It is part of the Science Centre's exhibition - 'Changing World'.
Photos on this page supplied by the Science Centre.

NAN TIEN

Rising majestically from Flagstaff Hill, adjacent to the F6 Freeway at Berkeley, Nan Tien is the largest Buddhist temple in the southern hemisphere. The temple is Australian headquarters of the Taiwanese-based Fo Kuang Shan Buddhist Order, which has 300 temples and branches worldwide and hundreds of millions of followers, including more than 30,000 in Australia. Meaning 'Mountain of Buddha's Light', Fo Kuang Shan espouses the idea of Buddhism for the human realm.

In response to lobbying by local Buddhists and encouragement from Wollongong City Council, Fo Kuang Shan's founder, the Venerable Master Hsing Yun, decided in 1990 that Wollongong, with its close proximity to Sydney, was an ideal site for the temple.

After years of planning and construction, the lavish $50 million Chinese-style temple opened amid great fanfare in October 1995. Melding East and West in design and finish, Nan Tien's startling saffron, terracotta and fuchsia colour scheme is traditional to Fo Kuang Shan. The main temple of the 22-hectare site is strategically positioned at equal angles between the mountain peaks of Mount Kembla and Mount Keira. Its magnificent roof structure, enclosed with more than 180,000 terracotta tiles, sweeps in curves from the eaves to the ridges, which are capped by dragons, seahorses, lions and deities. Surrounded by meticulously manicured gardens, complete with reflection ponds, the temple area is adorned with thousands of gold statues of Buddha.

Designed to become part of the wider Illawarra community, the temple complex has many halls, a library, a museum, dining rooms, dormitories and conference auditorium. Its multi-functional design allows it to serve as a place of worship and an educational and cultural centre. Nan Tien, which in English means Paradise of the South, attract more than 200,000 visitors each year, making it an important spiritual, educational and tourism centre for the region. While a path is open at Nan Tien for those who are interested in studying the teachings of Buddha, monks and nuns at the temple say their main wish is for Buddha's teachings to improve the everyday lives of Illawarra people and all Australians.

Left: The tapering eight-storey pagoda overlooking the Nan Tien Temple grounds has been erected to accommodate the cremated remains of departed worshippers.
Above right: An aerial view of the temple complex showing its proximity to Lake Illawarra and the ocean.
Right: The stunning colour scheme of the temple is traditional to Fo Kuang Shan.

SHELLHARBOUR

Explorers, graziers and cedar cutters visited Shellharbour from as early as 1796, yet it wasn't until the 1830's that Europeans began to settle the area. Cattle grazing dates back to 1803 and cedar cutters worked the district without permission from 1810. When rural pioneer and philanthropist Caroline Chisholm brought 23 families to Shellharbour in 1843 the population almost doubled overnight. By then, timber cutting licences had been introduced and new settlers were granted clearing leases that gave them about 50 hectares of natural bush. Each family was given seven, rent-free years to clear the land and establish a self-sufficient farm. Chisholm eventually settled immigrants on 1600 hectares around Shellharbour.

The name Shellharbour was in popular usage early during settlement and aptly described the shell remains of Aboriginal middens found around its shores.

During the 19th century, cedar, lime, wheat, cattle, coal (at Tongarra) and basalt were ultimately overshadowed by the area's thriving dairying industry.

Left: An aerial view of Windang Island and Warilla. Blackbutt Reserve, the Illawarra's last remaining stand of coastal plain forest, is evident in the middle ground and Shellharbour is visible beyond.
Below: The open air amphitheatre at Blackbutt Reserve.

Shellharbour - which includes the areas of Warilla, Oak Flats, Blackbutt and the fast-developing Albion Park - stretches from the southern side of Lake Illawarra and Macquarie Rivulet in the north to Macquarie Falls in the west and the Minnamurra River bordering Kiama in the south. No longer a centre for dairying, Shellharbour is a residential and recreational powerhouse that is highly regarded as a mecca for watersports.

The City of Shellharbour covers 154 square kilometres and its rapid population growth - the area is home to more than 60,000 people - is expected to continue through the first two decades of the 21st century, fuelled largely by the city's dynamic $1 billion Shell Cove residential development project. Now one of the most sought-after addresses in the Illawarra, Shell Cove is situated on a gentle hillside overlooking the Pacific Ocean. When complete it will boast 3200 residential lots, a 350-berth marina and inshore boat harbour, an elite-standard 18-hole golf course as well as commercial and tourist facilities.

Left: The pretty, sheltered harbour at Shellharbour.
Below: The Beverley Whitfield Pool, Shellharbour's sea-water swimming baths, are named in honour of local swimming legend Beverley Whitfield, who won Olympic and Commonwealth Gold medals for breast stroke.
Overleaf: An aerial view of Shellharbour.

KIAMA

While explorer George Bass is credited for making the first recorded reference to Kiama in 1797, the seaside village's first European settler was cedar cutter David Smith. Cedar dominated the economy in the early years, but once its supply was exhausted dairying started to thrive.

Keen to produce the best, through careful culling Kiama's pioneering dairymen developed the high milk yielding and hardy Illawarra Shorthorn breed of cattle from Ayrshire, Shorthorn and Devon stock. Australia's first co-operative butter factory was formed in the district and by 1869 had begun to export product overseas.

In the 1870's, basalt quarries began operation, eventually surpassing dairying in economic importance. Basalt (commonly called blue metal), is used for road and rail base and concrete manufacture, and continues to be quarried at Kiama.

Left: An aerial view of Stack Island and the Minnamurra River entrance. Jones Beach and Kiama Downs and are visible in the distance.
Below: The Memorial Arch in Hindmarsh Park on Kiama's main street, Terralong Street.

There is mixed opinion on the meaning of the name Kiama, with some historians believing it is derived from the Aboriginal Kiarama, thought to mean 'where the sea makes a noise'. Others say Kiama comes from the words Kiara Mia, meaning 'fertile district'. The first view associates the town's name to the Kiama Blowhole, one of the most distinct and famous attractions on the South Coast.

Situated on Blowhole Point near the Kiama lighthouse, this unusual rock formation on the edge of the ocean shoots spumes of sea water into the air as waves surge through a natural hole in the rock. The blowhole's amazing release of natural energy attract thousands of visitors annually.

Left: A south easterly swell makes a spectacular show at Kiama's Surf Beach.
Below: The foreshore park on Marsden Head where Kiama's Little Blowhole is located.
Right: Kiama's spectacular Blowhole attracts visitors from around the world. First reported by explorer George Bass, who thought it was the result of a volcanic eruption, the blowhole was, in fact, formed by the action of air in a sea-worn cave. Compressed by waves, air in the cave forces a vertical passage upwards, eventually breaking through any incoming wave, which is forced upwards to 'blow'.

Kiama Harbour, adjacent to the blowhole, is home to the local fishing fleet and game-fishing charter boats. The rocky coastal outcrops interspersed by golden beaches draw holiday makers and sightseers away from the pretty town's many specialty arts and crafts shops.

Bordered seawards by Norfolk Island pines, Kiama is both a popular tourist destination and a desirable place to live for retirees and commuters in the region.

Situated only 30 minutes south of the heart of Wollongong, the municipality covers 259 square kilometres from the Minnamurra River in the north to the Foxground boundary and the top of Jamberoo Pass in the west. Home to about 20,000 people, the area includes Australia's southernmost subtropical rainforest, Minnamurra, and the coastal villages of Gerringong and Gerroa to the south and the quaint village of Jamberoo nestled at the foot of the escarpment to the west.

Left: Blowhole Point, Kiama. The promontory is an excellent vantage point for viewing whales on their annual migration from July to October.
Below: Completed in 1876, Kiama Harbour once catered to the area's growing shipping trade. These days it is used by pleasure craft, commercial fishing vessels and the area's game-fishing and scuba diving charter boats.
Right: Stately Norfolk Pines are a feature of the Kiama foreshore.

JAMBEROO

The Jamberoo Valley was settled by Europeans in the 1820's. After land was cleared, grazing began and within 10 years the village of Jamberoo had become a thriving, bustling community surrounded by fertile dairy farms.

Landmarks around Jamberoo include seven pioneer cemeteries, Terragong House (a Georgian-style home built in 1858 by former Kiama mayor John Marks), local watering hole the Jamberoo Hotel (today's structure includes sections of the original 1857 building), Jamberoo Public School (built from local sandstone and cedar in 1878) and four churches dating from the 1860's.

A folk music festival that describes itself as 'the biggest little folk festival in the world' continues to draw big names and large crowds annually.

Thrillseekers also visit Jamberoo to enjoy one of the region's most popular tourist attractions, Jamberoo Recreation Park. Situated just a few kilometres north of the lush rural village and open all year round the parks attractions include mountain tobogganing, racing cars, water slides, a chairlift, golf and power boat rides. There's also a flower plantation and craft centre.

Elsewhere in Jamberoo visitors will find an 18-hole golf course, lawn bowls, a swimming pool and tennis courts. West of the village is Minnamurra Rainforest Park, part of Budderoo National Park, where boardwalks and an education centre promote visitors' enjoyment of the natural environment.

Left: Jerrara's so-called 'Australia Dam', on the road from Kiama to Jamberoo.
Above right: Jamberoo's dairy farming traditions are being threatened by the de-regulation of the dairy industry.
Right: Dating back to 1857, the Jamberoo pub is a local landmark.
Overleaf: An aerial view of the rural community of Jamberoo.

GERRINGONG

The coastal village of Gerringong, 10 minutes south of Kiama, is the perfect place to kick back and enjoy life at a slower pace. Surrounded by farmland and buttressed by ocean, mountains and national parkland, this idyllic escape is steeped in history and belies its Aboriginal name, thought to mean 'fearful place'. Still standing is the original 1876 police station, built from stone with walls 60 centimetres thick, as well as homesteads and cottages dating from the 1840's and four churches dating from 1874.

Gerringong's boat harbour, now popular with picnickers and boaties, was the site of the original 1851 jetty, once an important shipping link to Sydney.

Gerringong Golf Club's 18-hole, par-72 sea-side course is among the most picturesque courses in the region.

Left: Werri Beach and the seaside town of Gerringong.
Below: Dairy cows graze at Rose Valley.

Between the beaches and the escarpment, the lush and picturesque farmlands of Rose Valley, Foxground and Toolijooa continue the region's dairy farming traditions.

The award-winning Crooked River Winery and vineyard opened its doors in 1998. Situated south-west of the Gerringong township at Willow Vale Estate on 14 hectares of former dairy farm, the vineyard is planted with more than 31,000 vines. It is now the largest self-producing winery on the New South Wales South Coast - the youngest wine region in Australia. The commercial winery produces a range of reds and whites, including cabernet sauvignon, chambourcin, cabernet merlot and a verdelho chardonnay.

Left: Werri Beach is a famous surfing beach, attracting locals and holiday makers with its fantastic waves and picturesque surrounds.
Below: Majestic pines line the foreshore at Gerringong.

GERROA

Minutes south of Gerringong is the pretty coastal village of Gerroa, also popular with commuters, retirees and holidaymakers. The village is located on a headland at the northern end of Seven Mile Beach.

Survivors of the 1797 wreck of the Sydney Cove are thought to have been the first Europeans to set foot in the area. After returning to Sydney, these survivors' reports spurred George Bass to explore the region.

A memorial and lookout overlooking Seven Mile Beach commemorates aviator Sir Charles Kingsford Smith's second crossing of the Tasman to New Zealand in January 1933. Kingsford Smith chose a long, smooth stretch of Seven Mile Beach to begin his epic flight aboard the 'Southern Cross'. Thousands of onlookers flocked to the beach for Kingsford Smith's 2.30am take-off from a runway lit by flares and car headlights. Seventy years earlier the beach was used regularly for horse racing and in subsequent years car and bike races.

Left: The southernmost town in the Illawarra, Gerroa is perched on a headland overlooking Seven Mile Beach. In 1933 Sir Charles Kingsford Smith used the beach to commence his second crossing of the Tasman aboard his plane the 'Southern Cross'.
Below: Crooked River, Gerroa.

MINING AND INDUSTRY

The Illawarra's coal-smudged ocean cliffs were first reported in Sydney Town in 1797 by the survivors of the shipwrecked Sydney Cove. Excited by the potential discovery, Governor Hunter despatched George Bass to investigate. Although Bass returned with news of an extensive coal seam in the seaside cliffs of the northern Illawarra, the inaccessibility of the region meant that 40 years elapsed before a government geologist was sent to investigate the region's coal reserves.

In the meantime, extensive stands of cedar had been discovered and timber became the region's first industry. This was followed by dairying after Liverpool farmer Charles Throsby came to the district in 1815 in search of feed for his drought-stricken cattle.

After several failed attempts at mining coal outcrops in seaside cliffs, James Shoobert's Mount Keira colliery began operation in 1849. Shoobert's success signalled a new era, one that would change the region forever. Illawarra's coal industry suddenly began to look like a veritable gold mine - black and bottomless. More than a century later in the 1940's the region's coal reserves were estimated at 11,000 million tonnes and described as the highest grade coal in NSW.

More than 150 years later, records show that hundreds of men and boys have lost their lives in Illawarra mining disasters. In 1887 when pit conditions were primitive and the work was back-breaking a cave-in at Bulli colliery claimed 81 lives. Fifteen years later on the last day of July in 1902, Australia's worst mining disaster killed 95 men when a rock fall at the Mount Kembla colliery caused gases to ignite. The resulting explosion was heard eight kilometres away.

From 1850 onwards, new pits began to mushroom wherever high-grade coal was found and by 1880 ten mines were being worked around Wollongong and several mining villages had sprung up to the north. 'Black gold' had become the mainstay of the economy, servicing Sydney and Wollongong's energy needs and spawning new industry.

Long jetties used by ships that transported coal to Sydney and over-seas soon sprung up at headlands and beaches protected from strong southerly winds. As coal mining grew, the problems posed by the lack of a natural deep-water harbour became more obvious. It wasn't until 1861 that the colony's government finally began work to upgrade Wollongong Harbour at Belmore Basin. By 1895 more than 250,000 tonnes of cargo was departing Wollongong Harbour annually.

In 1888, the completed Illawarra-Sydney rail link suddenly fast-tracked the region's industrial development. This was further boosted at the turn of the 20th century when construction began on a larger port better suited to deep-sea ships and capable of future expansion. Port Kembla's close proximity to coal pits and road and rail transport made it an ideal site. By 1930 its two breakwaters enclosed a deepwater port of more than 130 hectares. Today Port Kembla remains one of Australia's largest bulk-commodity ports - in 2002/03 it shifted 22.7 million tonnes.

At Kiama, basalt was being quarried as the 19th century closed. The Illawarra's 'blue gold' was used in local buildings from the mid-1800's and was shipped to Sydney from 1870 onwards. Basalt mining began at Bass Point in Shellharbour 10 years later and continues to be mined in Shellharbour and Kiama.

In 1908 the region's first copper refinery opened, followed by a metal manufacturing factory and a fertiliser production plant. Yet it was Charles Hoskins' purchase of 162 hectares of land west of Port Kembla that ultimately dictated the direction of Illawarra industry. Hoskins' iron and steel works began producing steel in 1931. That same year, Hoskins merged with two British firms to become Australian Iron and Steel. In 1935, this company was sold to Broken Hill Proprietary Company Limited (BHP), which continued to expand into the 1950's. Another 640 hectares of land was bought and by 1939 there were five open hearth furnaces and a continuous billet mill producing steel slabs. Post-World War II the steelworks continued to boom and Port Kembla was ranked as Australia's largest industrial complex.

In 1946 the steelworks employed 3500 people. The move towards ethnic diversity began in the 1950's in response to massive expansion in the Australian steel industry. From the 1950's through the 1970's BHP

Left: The reclaimer unit at Port Kembla Coal Terminal transfers coal from the stock-pile onto a conveyor system, which in turn transfers the coal onto vessels destined for Japan, India, Korea, China or Europe.

maintained an itinerant, largely immigrant workforce drawn to the region by the promise of work and a rewarding life.

The workforce had doubled by 1953 and doubled again by 1961 when 15,000 workers were on the payroll and another 2000 worked at BHP collieries. By 1980, BHP's Illawarra operations had 23,000 employees. To remain competitive internationally, however, BHP had to embrace new cost-efficient technologies and shed labour.

Today BHP Billiton and BlueScope Steel Limited (formerly BHP Steel) employ about 12,000 people who live and work in the Illawarra. The scope of operations is considerable and includes slab and plate products, sheet and coil products, refractories, collieries, research, transport and engineering. Together these generate considerable wealth for the region and the nation.

Dendrobium, opened in November 2003, is BHP Billiton's latest mining project, and has the potential to be one of Australia's biggest underground mines, producing more than five million tonnes of coal a year.

While BHP Billiton is Australia's biggest company on the world stage and the region's undisputed industry leader, there are many other players that help make the Illawarra an economically dynamic community. Steel producer OneSteel, formerly owned by BHP, has contracts for the manufacture, coating and delivery of pipe for the Telfer Pipeline, North Queensland Gas Pipeline and Esperance Pipeline projects.

Collieries not owned by BHP Billiton operate at South Bulli and Helensburgh. The Corrimal and Illawarra Coke Works produce high-grade coking coal used at foundries and smelting plants across Australia and in South-East Asia. BOC Gases' Port Kembla extraction plant produces nitrogen, oxygen and argon in liquid form that is used for steel-making processes. Port Kembla Copper produces copper coil and extracts gold and silver in the manufacturing process. The Port Kembla Grain Terminal, located adjacent to the coal terminal at Port Kembla Harbour, handles grain from central and southern NSW to service billion-dollar export markets in the Middle East, Sri Lanka, Pakistan, China and the expanding South-East Asian markets of Malaysia, Indonesia and Thailand.

Left: An aerial view of the industrial heartland of Port Kembla, showing the Port Kembla Coal Terminal, the Port Kembla Grain Terminal and part of BHP Billiton's extensive steel-making operations.

In the region's south, basalt quarries operate in Shellharbour and Kiama. The blue metal produced is used as road base and for road surfacing. It is also used as railway ballast and in the manufacture of concrete.

Most of the Illawarra's industrial might is located within Australia's Industry World, regarded as the most spectacular industrial complex in the southern hemisphere. The 700-hectare site includes the BHP Steelworks Garden and the BHP Visitors' Centre, which features a scale model of the steelworks. From the centre visitors can take self-guided tours of the Grain Terminal, Coal Terminal and Tom Thumb Lagoon.

Left: A vessel is unloaded at Port Kembla Inner Harbour's ore unloading berth.
Above right: The Port Kembla Grain Terminal, commissioned in 1989, is one of the most highly automated grain terminals in the world.
Right: Boral's Basalt quarry at Dunmore

LIGHTSTORM PHOTO GALLERY

The Lightstorm Photo-Gallery in Berry displays an exciting collection of photographic prints by landscape photographers Sue and Brian Kendrick. Photographed largely on Linhof Master Technika and Art Panorama large format cameras, the collection features images from the Illawarra, the Shoalhaven and around Australia.

Many of the images featured in this book, plus others not shown, are available framed or unframed in a range of sizes. A selection of framing styles is available.
Some of the most striking images from the Lightstorm collection are available as signed and numbered Limited Edition Prints.

Albert Court, Albert Street, Berry NSW 2533
Gallery Ph: 02 4464 3165